First published in Belgium and Holland by Clavis Uitgeverij, Hasselt – Amsterdam, 2015
Copyright © 2015, Clavis Uitgeverij

English translation from the Dutch by Clavis Publishing Inc. New York
Copyright © 2015 for the English language edition: Clavis Publishing Inc. New York

Visit us on the web at www.clavisbooks.com

All About the Seasons written and illustrated by Mack
Original title: *Alles over seizoenen*
Translated from the Dutch by Clavis Publishing

ISBN 978-1-60537-203-7

This book was printed in February 2015 at Proost Industries NV, Everdongenlaan 23, 2300 Turnhout, Belgium

First Edition
10 9 8 7 6 5 4 3 2 1

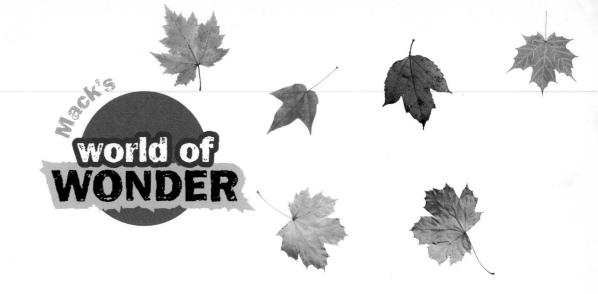

Mack's world of WONDER

ALL ABOUT THE SEASONS

Mack

Clavis

NEW YORK

Fall

STORM CLOUDS

IT IS FALL. It's getting colder outside. The sun hides behind dark clouds. Every now and then it appears again. *Whoosh! Whoosh!* It can get really windy in fall. **Storm clouds** gather. Sometimes, after the rain, you can see a beautiful rainbow.

When there is a storm,
the autumn trees sway
back and forth. Leaves
and umbrellas fly around.
Even the dog has difficulty
moving forward.
Woof, it's not easy!

Which animals like the wind? Which animals don't?

MAGICAL CARPETS

FALL LEAVES are beautifully colored. The trees turn from green to yellow, red or orange as if they were magical trees. Aren't they beautiful? At first the leaves stay on the tree, but that doesn't last long. A little breeze is all it takes to make them flutter through the sky. Then they land softly on the ground. The ground is orange and yellow, like a **magical carpet**.

Some trees stay green, even in fall. They don't have leaves on their branches, they have long thin needles instead. Just look at the Christmas tree!

Which are fall leaves?

GOLDEN ROLLS

The **WHEAT FIELDS** look very pretty in fall. The wheat grows from a little seed into a big stalk that is harvested in late summer and early fall. When it's harvested the wheat grain is collected and used to make bread and beer. The stalks are gathered into big rolls, called bales. In fall the bales of hay lie all over the fields. Look, in the fall sunshine they look like **golden rolls**!

Crows love wheat and
want to eat it. The farmer
isn't happy about that!
To scare the crows away
he makes a scarecrow.
But not every crow is
afraid....

Which tractor pulls the most wheat?

ORANGE GIANTS

PUMPKINS don't grow on trees or bushes. They grow on the ground. That makes sense because most pumpkins are very big, sometimes even bigger than your head. They get so big and heavy that a bush or a tree would fall over from their weight. In fall they are ready to be picked. You can make delicious soup or pie with those big **orange giants**.

Pumpkins come in all shapes and colors. Big and small. On Halloween the big orange pumpkins are used to make jack-o'-lanterns. Scary!

Which pumpkin looks a bit like a pear?

CRAWLY LITTLE CREATURES

SPIDERS like fall. They make the most beautiful webs then. Because of the rain this cobweb is full of little drops and you can see exactly how the spider made her web. Isn't it pretty? Spiders love to eat bugs. They catch their food in their webs – little flies, mosquitoes and other **crawly little creatures.**

In fall you can see all kinds of little critters crawling around. Snails, beetles and worms are all looking for food. Ladybirds also fill their stomachs in fall, because when cold winter comes, there won't be much food to be found.

Which snails are exactly the same?

FRUIT TREES

Apples grow on trees. Just like cherries and pears. In the spring beautiful little flowers appear between the green leaves. But in the summer those flowers become juicy little apples. At first the apples are green and small, but later they grow bigger. And in the fall they're ready to be picked. Then you can eat the yummy apples. Thanks, **fruit trees**!

Lots of animals enjoy a juicy apple too.
But the apples hang up high in the tree,
so they can't reach them. This goat managed
to get hold of an apple.
Enjoy it, little goat!

Which trees are apple trees and which are pear trees?

COLLECTORS

SQUIRRELS hop from tree to tree looking for food in fall. And what do they do when they find a nut? Sometimes they eat it immediately, but mostly they bury their food. Bury it? Yes, because winter is coming and there will be almost no food left. But squirrels don't have to worry. They just dig up the food they hid in fall. Squirrels are smart **collectors**.

In fall you can see squirrels climb the trees. Because there are so few leaves left on the trees the squirrels are easy to spot. Look, this one is jumping from tree to tree.

Is the squirrel's food underneath the first, the middle or the last tree?

FLYAWAYS

BIRDS fly through the sky as they migrate at the end of fall. Geese, storks, and many other birds fly to faraway countries in the south where it is summer and the sun is warm. If you look closely, you'll see that the birds fly in a 'V' shape. One bird is in front and the others spread out behind. That way they are protected from the wind, those **flyaways**.

Lots of birds think fall is too cold and fly away to warmer countries. But luckily not all birds go away. Some birds like the fall and stay here.

Birds need to eat a lot before winter starts. Which bird has the most to eat?

WINTER

SNOWSTORMS

IT IS WINTER. Brr, it's very cold outside! The sun hides behind dark, gray clouds and hardly shows itself. Soft white snowflakes fall out of the clouds. In winter it can also be windy. Very windy. The wind blows the snow in all directions. Everything turns white in those fierce **snowstorms**.

It's fun to play in the snow. You can make a beautiful snowman. Hello, snowman! Little animals like snow too. They hide behind heaps of snow. Can you see the rabbit?

Which snowmen are exactly the same?

SUGAR TREES

THE TREES look very different in winter. All the leaves have fallen from the branches and the trees are completely bare. They can look sad without their green leaves. But sometimes, when it's extremely cold outside, the trees are more beautiful than ever. Everything freezes and turns white: the grass, the bushes and the trees too. They look like **sugar trees**.

The sun isn't very warm
in winter: it hides behind
the clouds or stays very
low on the horizon,
behind the trees.
That's why the snow
doesn't melt right away!

Which tree belongs in winter?

EVERGREENS

CONIFERS are really prickly. They have needles on their branches, not leaves. Be careful, because they are sharp. Ouch! The prickly needles like the wind and the cold. They hold on tight to the branches of the trees and don't fall off. That's why conifers are beautifully green in winter.
They are real **evergreens.**

The Christmas tree
is a conifer too and
stays green in winter.
They're not only
green though, because
Christmas trees
are decorated with
colorful ornaments
and ribbons, and often
have a bright star on
the top.

Which Christmas tree has the most lights?

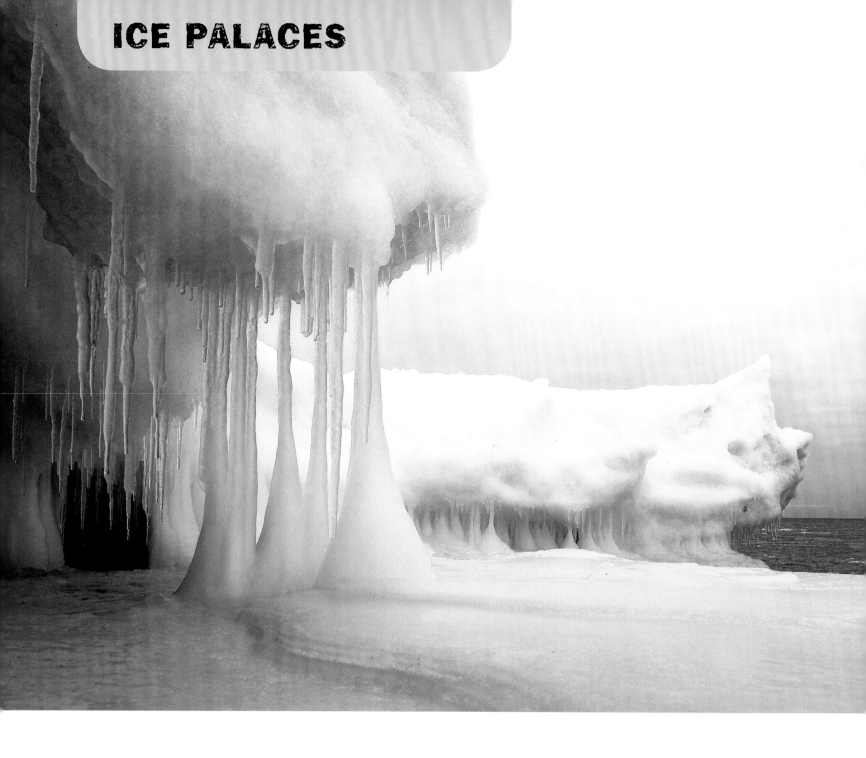

ICE PALACES

WATER changes into ice when it's really cold. Water that trickles down freezes in the air and becomes solid. The water drops look like popsicles. Unfortunately, they are not as delicious as the real ones. The ice is very beautiful, though, and it can become very thick because of the cold. That's why, once in a while, you can see real **ice palaces**.

Sculptors can make beautiful works of art with ice. Look at this magnificent ice castle! When it gets warmer, the castle will melt into a pool of water.

How many rabbits are hiding behind the blocks of ice?

FROZEN VEGETABLES

CABBAGES grow well in winter. They grow from small to quite large before they are ready to be picked. Most vegetables, like tomatoes, lettuce, and cucumbers don't like the cold, but cabbages do! They taste best when it's freezing outside. They are real **frozen vegetables**.

Cabbages can stand the cold, but berries and fruit need to be picked before winter starts. If you're too slow, the fruit falls on the ground and rots.

Carrots that grow in winter are much bigger than average carrots. Can you see them?

HORSES grow thicker coats in winter. That protects them against the cold – just like a real winter jacket. That way, they don't suffer from the cold. Even if it's snowing or freezing, horses stay nice and warm in their **winter coats**.

Just like horses, sheep have thick woollen winter coats. They like to stand together in a flock. That way they help keep each other warm.

When it's very cold, horses are covered with a blanket. Which one has the longest blanket?

ROBINS don't find much to eat in winter. Just like many other birds robins like insects such as flies, but when it's cold there are no flies. Because birds have little to eat in winter, they get cold easily. When it's freezing and snowing, they have a tough time. You often see Robins shivering on a branch. Poor **shiverers**!

It's easy to help birds in wintertime. They need food and love seeds and nuts. If you put those in a bird feeder a lot of birds will visit your yard.

How many birds have found food?

WINTER SLEEPERS

BEARS get really tired from all the cold. Before winter starts, they eat as much food as they can. Then they search for a warm cave or they dig a big hole in the ground. When it gets really cold outside, they hide in their new homes. They sleep until it gets warmer again. That's a long snooze! Bears are real **winter sleepers**!

Bears are not the only animals to nap in winter. Many other animals sleep too. They don't sleep for just an hour or a night, they sleep the whole winter long until it gets warm again. Sleep tight!

Bats sleep in wintertime too, but some of these bats are still awake. Which ones?

SPRING

SUNBEAMS

IT IS SPRING. The cold winter has passed and it's getting warmer again. Yippee! The sun is shining, the grass is turning the freshest green, and the sky is changing from dark gray into beautiful blue. In spring everything looks like one big party. Colorful flowers shoot out of the ground, trees are covered with fresh leaves and there are baby animals everywhere! Everything and everyone enjoys the first delightful **sunbeams**.

The meadows are filled with  beautiful flowers. The little rabbit has found a dandelion. When you blow on the puff, you can make a wish. What would a little rabbit wish? A carrot maybe?

In spring, many animals have babies. Which baby animals do you see here?

FLOWERING TREES

TREES look very beautiful in spring. Their branches are completely covered with little blossoms that give them marvelous colors. One tree turns white, another one pink. After a while the flowers fall on the ground and are replaced by delicious fruit: a fresh apple or a juicy pear.

Do you know what trees with blossoms are called? **Flowering trees**.

All day long, bees fly from blossom to blossom. *Zoom, zoom, zoom!* Only when the bees have passed by do blossoms change into fruit. Without bees we wouldn't have any delicious fruit. Thank you very much, bees!

Which fruit grows from a pink blossomed tree? And which fruit from a white one?

JUICY LEAVES

FORESTS turn different colors all year long. In summer the trees are green, in fall brown, orange and red, and in winter they are completely bare. A bare forest is a bit sad to see. That's why everyone is so happy when spring comes and the forest is more beautiful than ever. Magnificent green plants rise from the ground and trees grow **juicy leaves**.

Do you know how plants grow? They start under the ground as little seeds. The seeds grow roots and develop into green plants above the ground. *Yummy,* the horse thinks!

In spring, the leaves are light green. Which are spring leaves?

SNUFFLING NOSES

RABBITS have lots of babies in spring. If you look carefully, you'll see many fields are filled with little jumping rabbits. Baby rabbits are born in burrows, but as soon as the sun shines, they go out. They have to be brave! Sometimes the little animals are a bit afraid and Mommy rabbit has to tempt them to come out. Soon they are all outside, though, those cute **snuffling noses**!

Rabbits don't walk, they jump. *Hop, hop, hop.* They move through the grass until they see a flower. Then they stop and smell. Yummy, what a sweet smell!

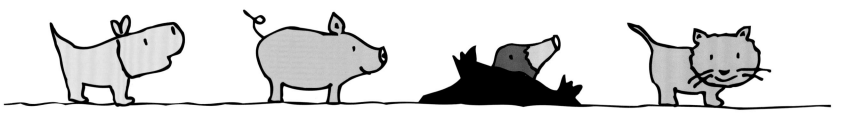

Which animal lives underground?

GREEN PEAS grow from plants. Long green pods with green peas inside hang from the plants. In the beginning you can hardly see the peas. They are very little and hide in the beans. But when they grow, the pods crack open and the green peas fall out ready to be eaten. Have a nice meal!
Yummy, such delicious **spring vegetables**.

There are many peas in the pods of pea plants. Sometimes there are six, seven or even eight peas in a pod. When you open the pod, the peas roll out, right into the bowl. How convenient!

Which spoon contains the most peas?

YELLOW FLUFFIES

DUCKLINGS come out of their eggs when the sun is shining bright and it gets warmer again. In the beginning they stay close to each other and walk in a straight line. When one moves, the others follow immediately. That's how they waddle over the grass – one after the other. Ducklings stick together in the water too. How cute they look, those **yellow fluffies**!

Baby ducks walk from the waterside into the pond and can swim immediately. In the beginning, Mommy duck watches to make sure they're safe. One duck is hesitating. First it touches the water. Wow, that's wet!

Which duck still has to learn how to walk?

RETURNING BIRDS

GEESE can swim and fly. They make very long journeys in small groups. Before winter begins, they fly into the sky and travel over forests, mountains and seas until they find the sun. In spring they fly back over seas, mountains and forests until they're home again. In spring, geese are **returning birds**.

Birds always look happy in spring. They twitter and chirp for hours on end. And they do the same when they are looking for a partner to build a nest with. *Chirp, chirp!*

Which babies belong to the mommy bird?

CURLY HEADS

LAMBS are usually born in spring, when the weather is nice and the meadows are full of fresh grass. Little sheep are fond of grass, which makes them grow. When they're not eating, lambs jump about cheerfully. They look very cute with their big ears, soft snouts and wobbly legs. Their fur is completely made of wool. They are real **curly heads**.

When lambs are born, they drink milk from their mothers. It takes a while before they start to eat grass. Later, when it's warmer, lambs are shorn. They look so funny when they are bald.

Which is not a natural color for a lamb?

SUMMER

ORANGE SKIES

IT IS SUMMER. Phew, it's so hot! The sun shines almost every day in summer. During the day the sun is high up in the sky. Later in the evening the sun goes down. Slowly it gets darker and everything changes color. The sky turns from blue to orange and red. Aren't they beautiful, those summer **orange skies** in summer?

Look, this little dog is happily digging holes at the beach.
Sea gulls also love the beach. And when they get too hot, they shelter from the sun. Look at that one keeping cool in the shade of the umbrella!

Which animals do you see here, swimming in the sea?

SUNFLOWERS

ONE FLOWER looks a bit like the sun. It only grows in the summer and has a very long stalk. This stalk can grow taller than four or five children standing on top of one another! At the end of the long stalk is a beautiful, yellow flower that looks at the sun. Do you know what this flower is called? You guessed it: **a sunflower.**

Everybody loves sunflowers! Many artists have painted the beautiful yellow flowers. Birds love the flowers too. They eat the seeds!

One sunflower is a bit sad. Which one?

RED BALLS

TOMATO PLANTS love a nice, hot sun. In the summer the plants grow and grow. And then suddenly – the plant is full of tomatoes! On some plants the tomatoes hang one by one, on others there's a whole bunch of them. Sometimes you see bunches of four or five bright red tomatoes hanging together. Those delicious **red balls** are tasty and healthy. Yum!

Small tomatoes are green, but when they grow bigger they change color. The tomatoes first become orange and then bright red. Red tomatoes are ready for eating. They are deliciously sweet and fresh!

Which vegetables do you see here?

KINGS OF SUMMER

STRAWBERRIES grow on little plants with thin stalks. The strawberry grows bigger in the summer, and the thin stalk slowly bends. From the stalk grow more beautiful red strawberries as well as little white flowers. And do you see the small yellow seeds on the strawberry? It's from those seeds new strawberry plants will grow next summer. Strawberries really are the **kings of summer.**

You can eat strawberries on their own, but you can also use them to decorate a cake. With a few cherries, raspberries and berries from the garden, you can make a delicious summer cake. Put some whipped cream on top. *Yum, yum!*

Which strawberry has the most seeds?

PURPLE FIELDS

FLOWERS are everywhere in the summer. On the side of the roads, in fields, and in gardens the flowers bloom in the most beautiful colors: red, white, yellow or even purple. Those purple flowers are called lavender. Mm, lavender smells really good. So good that we make soap and bath oil with it. Lavender grows in beautiful **purple fields.**

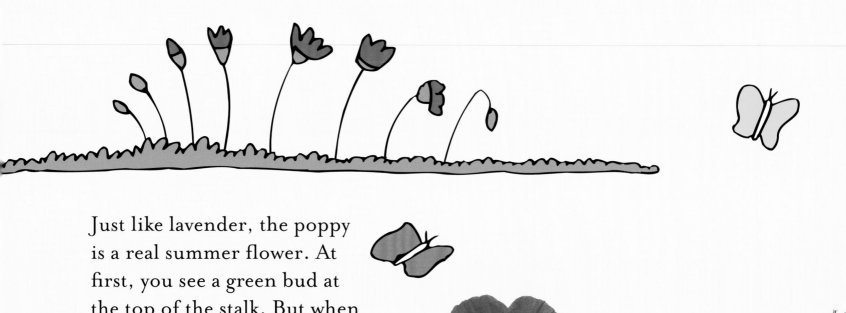

Just like lavender, the poppy is a real summer flower. At first, you see a green bud at the top of the stalk. But when it gets warmer, a beautiful flower appears. Butterflies and bees love those beautifully colored poppies.

There are different kinds of poppies. Which colors do you see here?

TODDLER ANIMALS

ON THE FARM new animals are born in spring. In the summer those little ones grow to be toddlers. They're big enough to stand on their own four legs and they learn something new every day. This little pig, for instance, just learned how to look for food all by himself. They all have to learn new things, those cute **toddler animals**.

Little lambs, calves, chicks, little goats and funny piglets, it's very busy on the farm in summer! This foal still has very thin legs and isn't ready to stand up. "Come on, get up," Mommy horse says. "You can do it."

Which pig doesn't have a curly tail?

BEACH ANIMALS

CRABS live in the sea. In summer they often appear on the beach. You can see them walking sideways. Silly, eh? Can you do that too, walk sideways like a crab? Try it, it's pretty hard! Crabs are so good at it, they even run sideways on the sand. Just like starfish and sea urchins, crabs are **beach animals**.

You can find the prettiest things and animals on the beach: shells, mussels, starfish and jellyfish. If you're very lucky, you might even see a baby seal. Seals are born on the quietest parts of the beach.

Starfish have five arms or more. Are these all starfish?

LAZYBONES

BEARS lead a life of ease. They sleep all winter long. But if you think that after all that snoring they go running around in the summer, you're mistaken. When the first rays of sunshine appear you can see the bears sighing and puffing as they walk to the water. Time for some quiet bobbing up and down in the river. Bears are real **lazybones.**

Bears can sleep anywhere, any time. They don't need a bed. They just plop down on the grass. This one can barely keep his eyes open while leaning on a tree stump. Sweet dreams, mister bear!

Bears are excellent swimmers. Can you see which bear caught a fish?

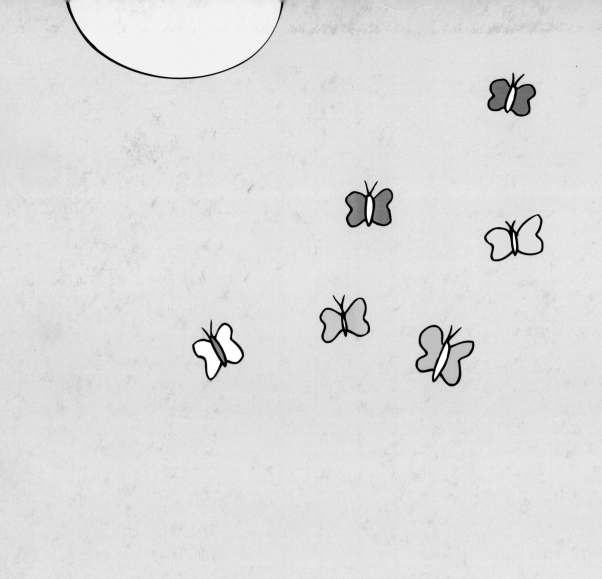